Immigration
A Scholastic Curriculum Guide

BY Tara McCarthy

SCHOLASTIC
PROFESSIONAL BOOKS

NEW YORK • TORONTO • LONDON • AUCKLAND • SYDNEY
MEXICO CITY • NEW DELHI • HONG KONG

Table of Contents

Cover design: Jaime Lucero
Cover photo: George Eastman House Collection
Interior design: Grafica, Inc.
Interior illustrations: Allan Eitzen
Photo research: Chantille Harris-Jenkins, Sarah Longacre

ISBN: 0-590-37950-X
Copyright © 1998 Scholastic
All rights reserved.

Introduction

LAUNCHING THE THEME

While this guide focuses on the massive immigration to the United States during the 19th and early 20th centuries, students should be able to relate to the concept of immigration, because all of them can trace their origins back to "somewhere else." From the first arrivals (Native American/Indian groups whose ancestors slowly immigrated across land bridges from Asia thousands of years ago), to the colonists who arrived here in the 16th-18th centuries, to the newest arrivals who came here only weeks ago from nations all over the world, we make up a nation of immigrants.

Use the stories and other materials here to help students see how they and their ancestors became part of this nation and how immigration continues to shape the United States.

GETTING STARTED

As you plan your study, you'll need to:

1. Set instructional goals. Decide on your objectives: What <u>facts</u> and <u>skills</u> do you want students to learn? What <u>affective</u> <u>understandings</u> do you hope they'll acquire?

2. Select on-target materials. Supply fiction and nonfiction books that provide a rich set of resources for facts and ideas and that suit different reading levels and individual interests. (You'll find a list of books on page 48.) Be sure to include some of the many pictorial, video, and audio materials available on this subject.

3. Create an engaging display of materials. On page 9, you'll find ideas for setting up an Interview Center.

4. Choose a rousing opener. Bring the class together and introduce the topic by reading aloud a book such as *Call Me Ruth* by Marilyn Sachs. Or, have volunteers take turns reading aloud some paragraphs from *If Your Name Was Changed at Ellis Island* by Ellen Levine. Aim for books that focus on the subject, provide needed background, and offer a taste of what else students can learn.

5. Make organizing webs work for you. You'll find a sample web on page 6 of this guide and a blank reproducible web on page 7.

GETTING MOTIVATED

1. Summon prior knowledge. Find out what students already know about immigration. Start a large K-W-L (Know/Want to Know/Learn) chart on tag-board or poster paper to keep on display. Begin with what students <u>Know</u>. As your study of immigration proceeds, fill in the **W** and **L** columns. Pass out copies of the reproducible K-W-L chart on page 8. Consider having students complete one of these individual charts each week so that they can track their acquisition of knowledge.

2. Provide needed background. Use the activities on pages 10-23 to give students basic information about immigration and to help them apply this information independently.

3. Stimulate interest in the human drama of immigration. Provide stories such as these from the descendants of immigrants. Discussion prompts: *What do you learn from these words? Why do American families like to keep these stories?*

Crossing-Over Melodrama

My grandfather came to America in about 1906 or so. Apparently he came either on a freighter or in steerage on a passenger ship...from Germany to New Orleans. There was a big storm at sea and he was washed overboard by one wave, but almost before he knew what was happening, another wave came and washed him back.

—Frederick L. Keppler, Washington, D.C.

Tiny Feet

There's just two stories I know about my great-great-grandmother, Nancy. She was Irish, and she came across during one of the potato famines. Apparently she cried so loud on the boat that the captain threatened to throw her overboard. The other story is that her feet were so tiny that she could do an Irish jig on a silver platter.

—Nancy Kilczewski, Herndon, Virginia

One Last Goodbye

When [my grandmother] left Russia during the Russian Revolution, they had soldiers out after her and my grandfather. They had just gotten married, and most of his older brothers and sisters had been in this country for a while, so he wanted to come here.

They escaped one night with my grandfather's father. They ran across the military lines, and they were shot at. And when they were at their destination, my grandmother decided that she didn't like the way she left. She wanted to go back to say goodbye to her family, because she knew she wouldn't be seeing them again, so she ran back through these military lines, and they shot at her again.

She said her goodbyes. Then she came back through, and they got on the boat, the three of them, and came over.

—Vicki Perler, Gaithersburg, Maryland

MANAGING THE UNIT

1. Describe the project. Explain that students will be using many different pieces of information to answer W-H questions about immigration. **Who** immigrated? **When** did they immigrate? **Why** did they immigrate? **Where** did they settle? **What** did they achieve? **How** has immigration shaped the American nation?

2. Model each process. Because students may be working independently on many segments of the unit, you'll want to make sure they understand how to proceed on their own for each assignment. For each task, model a strategy for students to follow. In some cases, you may have to model more than once.

3. Introduce peer-response journals. On these double-column pages, a student records reactions to books or activities, then has a partner respond to those comments. The strategy gives students immediate feedback, helps them take responsibility for their own learning, and provides a resource for student projects. At the same time, the strategy frees you from having to check each student's work on a daily basis. Once a week, you can confer with partners about their journals to make suggestions and informal assessments.

4. Schedule lessons and activities. In this guide, you'll find many suggestions for ways to promote learning. Study the Table of Contents and create a general, flexible schedule to guide you as you present critical thinking skills, the readers' theater play, literature circles, poetry, and projects.

> **Book: *If Your Name Was Changed at Ellis Island***
>
> | MY COMMENTS | MY PARTNER'S RESPONSE |
> | --- | --- |
> | pages 64–65 This is a lot like today! I only spoke Korean when I came to America. | Is it hard to learn a new language? What were the first English words you learned? |

5. Keep a daily Big Ideas Record. Help students collect and synthesize their knowledge of immigration by developing a display chart to record major ideas the class explores each day. Suggest that students use the chart as they write in their peer-response journals, plan upcoming projects, or assimilate new information with yesterday's learnings.

IMMIGRATION: BIG IDEAS		
DAY 1 All Americans came here from someplace else.	**DAY 2** Big tides of immigration took place in the 19th and early 20th centuries. Another huge tide of immigration is taking place now.	**DAY 3** Why immigrants come to America: poverty, adventure, persecution, famine, war, forced labor

6. Keep logs. Have students keep logs to note special resources they use in their study.

Organizing Web for Stories Related to Theme

The web below suggests a way to use books to focus on major immigrant groups. On page 7 of this guide, you'll find a blank organizing web that you can use for the books you and your students read. See page 48 for additional titles.

FROM ASIA
+ *Dragon's Gate* (F)
+ *The Star Fisher* (F)
+ *Angel Child, Dragon Child* (F)
+ *Everybody Cooks Rice* (F)
+ *Hoang Anh* (NF)

FROM LATIN AMERICA
+ *Hello Amigos!* (F)
+ *Everybody Cooks Rice* (F)

FROM EASTERN EUROPE
+ *Call Me Ruth* (F)
+ *Journey to America* (F)

Immigration

FROM WESTERN EUROPE
+ *So Far from Home* (F)
+ *When Hitler Stole Pink Rabbit* (F)
+ *The Long Way to a New Land* (F)

GENERAL
+ *Across America on an Emigrant Train* (NF)
+ *New Kids in Town* (NF)
+ *Train to Somewhere* (NF)
+ *Immigrant Kids* (NF)
+ *If Your Name Was Changed at Ellis Island* (NF)

(NF=Nonfiction; F=Fiction)

Scholastic Curriculum Guide: *Immigration*

Name: _____

Organizing Web

From Asia

From Latin America

From Eastern Europe

From Western Europe

Immigration

Other Places

General

Name: _____

My K-W-L Chart

What do you already know or think you know about immigration to the United States? Fill in the first column of the chart. In the second column, write what you want to find out. Save the chart. In the third column, write what you learn as you study immigration.

Immigration		
WHAT I *KNOW*	**WHAT I *WANT* TO KNOW**	**WHAT I *LEARNED***

Scholastic Curriculum Guide: *Immigration*

SETTING UP A RESOURCE CENTER:

Interview Center

B y setting up an Interview Center in your classroom, you not only build a central location for materials about immigration, but also provide a "stage setting" where—at different points in their study—students can play the roles of inspectors and immigrants. Students can also present or reenact interviews with neighbors or family members who are recent immigrants (see page 41).

SET THE STAGE

1. **Arrange the Interview Center near the classroom computer.** If students have access to the Internet, they will find much relevant material on immigration Web sites.

2. **Clear off a table or bookcase for your immigration materials.** If students will be borrowing materials, provide a sign-up/due-date register.

3. **Include a desk and a chair for the "inspector."**

4. **Provide bulletin boards and shelves for visuals.**

CREATE VISUALS FOR THE CENTER

1. **With students, make a poster** that lists key questions that immigrants must answer. Ask students to use the book *If Your Name Was Changed at Ellis Island* or the reproducible on page 17 of this guide as a source of questions an inspector might ask.

2. **Display a political world map for reference.**

3. **Expand the visuals with students' contributions.** Examples:
   - Adjacent to the question-poster, place empty dialogue balloons for students to fill with typical answers of immigrants at different periods of history.

   - Encourage students to bring in and display objects and mementos that represent the immigrant background of their own families. Students can write explanatory labels on index cards.

ENCOURAGE SHARING OF IDEAS AND RESOURCES

In the Center, provide an add-on log of resources such as the one here on which students can list helpful new materials they find.

Note that this log can provide you, the teacher, with a quick, informal assessment of students' independent research.

TITLE OF RESOURCE: _____

TYPE (book, video, web site)**:** _____
_____

HOW RESOURCE IS USEFUL ("Tells how names got changed." "Good timeline about tides of immigration.")**:** _____
_____

STUDENT'S NAME: _____

Tides of Immigration

To help students see how the United States has become "a nation of immigrants" in a relatively brief period of historical time, draw a time line, shown here, on the chalkboard. Also display a world map.

20,000 B.C.   1000 A.D. 2000 A

20,000 B.C.   First people came to America over Bering Strait

1000 A.D.   Vikings, from Scandinavia, explore Canada

1000 A.D.   1500 A.D.   2000 A.D.

1000–1492   Very little exploration and immigration

1492–1776   Europeans arrive. Most of them are English speaking. Enslaved people from Africa arrive.

1776–1924   Immigrants arrive from all over the world. Examples: Germany, Great Britain, Ireland, Norway, Sweden, Denmark, China, Japan, Italy, Russia, Spain, Poland, Greece, Hungary, Portugal

Ask students to refer to the time line as they respond to the following discussion prompts and questions. Note that students' responses allow you an informal strategy for assessing what they know, what they want to know and—for your instructional purposes—what they need to know.

1. Find the Bering Strait on the map. Where did the first Americans come from? Who are these first Americans today? For how many years have their ancestors been here?

2. Who was the European explorer who landed in America in 1492? Who came to America in the next 300 years? Did all the newcomers come here voluntarily?

3. Why did English become the all-purpose language of America?

4. Focus on the time-period 1776-1924. Encourage students to use prior knowledge:

   ✦ Why did people come to America from these countries?

   ✦ What problems might these immigrants have encountered when they arrived in the United States?

5. Focus on students' individual experiences and backgrounds:

   ✦ Did your family come to America in one of the time periods shown on this graph? If so, which one?

   ✦ Did your family immigrate to America in a time period <u>not</u> shown? If so, about when did they come? From where did they come?

Name: _____

Skills:
Using a Graph and Chart

Use the graph and the chart to answer these questions. If you wish, you can refer to a world map to help you find answers.

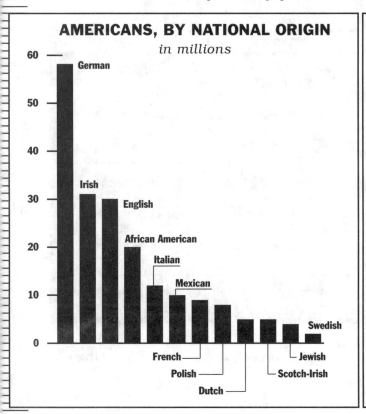

AMERICANS, BY NATIONAL ORIGIN
in millions

German, Irish, English, African American, Italian, Mexican, French, Polish, Dutch, Scotch-Irish, Jewish, Swedish

IMMIGRANTS TO U.S. (1991-1993)

PART OF WORLD	NUMBER OF IMMIGRANTS
Asia: Philippines, China, Vietnam, Korea, Hong Kong, India	494,078
Americas: Dominican Republic, El Salvador, Haiti, Jamaica, Mexico, Canada	1,708,410
Europe: Former USSR, Poland, United Kingdom	256,833

1. How many national origins are shown on the graph? _____

2. According to the graph, from which part of the world do most Americans today trace their origin? _____

3. Look at the chart. From which part of the world did most immigrants come between 1991 and 1993? _____ From which part did the fewest immigrants come? _____

4. Make your own prediction. By the middle of the 21st century, how might the graph change? _____

_____

Goals and Motives

To help students understand the major tides and motives for immigration beween 1840-1920, use this procedure:

1. Copy the following chart on the chalkboard or reproduce it for the overhead projector. Don't write the underlined sentences and phrases yet: these are examples of students' responses to write down as the discussion proceeds.

WHEN	WHO	SITUATION	WHY EMIGRATE?
1840s-1850s	Irish	Famine resulting from failure of potato crop	To find food
1840s-1880s	Germans	Unemployment; wars	To find jobs; to get away from wars
1870s-1900s	Norwegians, Danes, Swedes	Shortage of farmland	To find new farmland
1880s-1920s	Poles	Poverty; an outbreak of cholera	To find jobs; escape illness
1880s-1920s	Jews from Eastern Europe	Religious persecution	To be able to worship freely
1880s-1920s	Austrians, Czechs, Hungarians, Slovaks, Italians	Poverty, overpopulation	To find jobs
1910-1920s	Mexicans	Unemployment; wars	To find jobs; to get away from wars

2. As you show the chart, use prompts and questions that encourage affective as well as factual interpretations. Examples:

Factual:

+ What major groups arrived in the United States between the 1840s and the 1920s?

+ What were the main situations that made life in their home countries difficult for these newcomers?

Affective/Interpretive:

+ Imagine yourself as part of one of the immigrant groups shown on the chart. What would you be hoping to find if you came to America? (Enter students' responses in the last column on the chart. Sample responses are underlined.)

+ What did the immigrants have in common? How do you think they were different from one another? different from Americans who had arrived many years before them? different from immigrants today?

Scholastic Curriculum Guide: *Immigration*

Vocabulary of Immigration

As students learn about immigration, they will encounter terms related to it. The starter list that follows shows categories that you and your class can use. Encourage students to add to the lists.

ACTIVITIES

✦ Have students enter the terms and their meanings in a vocabulary notebook. Ask students to complete each entry with an original sentence using the term.

✦ Stretch shelf paper across a classroom wall and have students create a Word Wall.

✦ Have students write each word and its meaning on an index card and place the cards in the Interview Center.

✦ Challenge students to use the words as the basis of a word riddle game. For example: *I begin with a prefix which means "to remove." I mean "banish" or "expel." (deport)*

✦ Assign the reproducible puzzle on page 14 of this guide.

NAMES FOR PEOPLE AND GROUPS	NAMES FOR THINGS THAT HAPPEN	GOVERNMENT AND OFFICIAL TERMS
alien	assimilate	Ellis Island
illegal alien	immigrate	Angel Island
immigrant	emigrate	Immigration and Naturalization Service
ethnic group	deport	quota system
native	naturalize	visa
displaced person	persecution	green card
permanent resident	famine	national origin
citizen		
refugee		

Name: _____

Clues to Use Puzzle

Read each clue. Find the letters to spell the clue in one of the words about immigration in the box. *Hint: the boldface letters will help you.* Then write a sentence using both the clue and its immigration word. Try to link the meaning of the words. The first one is done for you.

naturalization	persecution	native
immigrated	assimilate	alien
green card	Angel Island	emigrated

Clues   **Immigration Words**

1. smile   assimilate
Try to smile as you learn to assimilate in this new place.

2. tie   _____

_____

3. gate   _____

_____

4. in   _____

_____

5. read   _____

_____

6. land   _____

_____

7. eat   _____

_____

8. turn   _____

_____

9. run   _____

Photos and Facts

S hare the pictures and information on these pages with students. Then provide students with copies of the interview form on page 17 of this guide. Have students work with a partner to complete the activity.

▲ In 1892, the U.S. government opened an Immigration Center on Ellis Island in New York Harbor. For the next 30 years, most immigrants came through Ellis Island. But there were also about 70 other immigration centers in other U.S. ports, such as in Boston, Galveston, Philadelphia, New Orleans, and San Francisco.

▲ From the 1820s until 1924, nearly 35 million people immigrated to America from Europe and Asia. Most of them had very little money and brought only the baggage they could carry. In addition, many immigrants could not speak English and did not have a definite job or place to live in the New World.

▲ Most immigrants passed through inspection at Ellis Island in about four hours. However, at Angel Island in San Francisco, Chinese immigrants might be detained for weeks and even years! This was because of an 1882 law that restricted the number of people that could come to the U.S. from China. For many Chinese immigrants, Angel Island was more like a prison than an immigrant interview center.

◀ As immigrant ships pulled into New York Harbor, the first sight passengers saw was the Statue of Liberty. The statue was a gift from France to honor the 100th anniversary of the founding of the United States. Emma Lazarus, a New York poet, wrote the poem engraved on the statue's pedestal. The most famous lines of the poem begin, "Give me your tired, your poor,/Your huddled masses yearning to breathe free..."

Facts

UNWILLING IMMIGRANTS

Not all immigrants came to America willingly. Examples:

- ✦ Between 1619, and well into the 1800s, hundreds of thousands of people were kidnapped from Africa, brought to America, and forced to work as slaves.

- ✦ People in England who had been convicted of crimes were often sent to British colonies like America to serve their terms in forced labor.

MAJOR STEPS FOR WILLING IMMIGRANTS

Show That You're Healthy

- ✦ Before they left their home ports, emigrants were examined for illnesses that would prevent their entry into the United States.

- ✦ At U.S. Immigration centers, people entering were again examined for physical diseases and mental problems. Sick people were detained for treatment, or in some cases sent back to their home countries.

Show That You Can Support Yourself

- ✦ Inspectors asked each immigrant between 20 and 30 questions. Many of the questions were about the immigrant's ability to make a living in the United States: could the immigrant support himself or herself without becoming a "public charge"?

Show That You Are Literate

- ✦ In 1917, Congress passed a literacy law for immigrants over the age of 16. The immigrant didn't have to know English, but did have to be able to read and write in some language.

Sent Back! (Deported)

About 5% of immigrants were sent back to the countries they'd come from. Reasons for deportation:

- ✦ an incurable or contagious disease
- ✦ a mental or physical problem that made someone unable to work
- ✦ a crime committed in the old country
- ✦ no skills for supporting oneself
- ✦ a job promised in America

The last two considerations were especially sticky ones for immigrants as inspectors interviewed them. (See page 17, Tips Questions 6 and 7.)

Name: _____

Interview Center Form

Inspectors asked each immigrant between 20 and 30 questions. Listed here are seven main questions. Below the questions are some Tips for Immigrants. With a partner, act out an interview between an immigration inspector and an immigrant. Write the immigrant's responses.

Inspector's Questions   **Immigrant's Answers**

1. What is your name? _____

2. Where were you born? _____

3. What country are you coming from? _____

4. How much money do you have with you? _____

   Do you have relatives in America? _____

5. If so, where do they live? _____

   _____

6. What job skills do you have? _____

7. Have you been promised a job in America? _____

Tips for Immigrants

Question 4: You have to have at least 10 dollars, plus money for railroad tickets if you are going beyond the port of entry.

Questions 6 and 7: Answer these questions carefully! You <u>have</u> to have a job skill, such as carpentry or sewing. <u>But</u>, you cannot have a job waiting for you! You might take lower wages than American workers and thus take jobs away from people already living here.

Responding to Primary Sources

T he excerpts below are the words of immigrants from Eastern Europe or of people who observed them. Share the passages with the class, then use the questions to help students appreciate the rigors of the immigrant experience.

LEAVING HOME: A FAMILY WAITS AT ANTWERP, GERMANY FOR A SHIP TO AMERICA. THEY MUST ALL BE EXAMINED BY A DOCTOR.

The doctor examines them and finds they are all hale and hearty and can go to America, but she, Goldele, cannot go, because she has trachomas on her eyes. At first her family did not understand. Only later did they realize it. That meant they could all go to America but she, Goldele, would have to remain here, in Antwerp. So there begins a wailing, a weeping, a moaning. Three times her mama fainted. Her papa wanted to stay here, but he couldn't. All the ship tickets would be lost. So they had to go off to America and leave her, Goldele, here until the trachomas would go away from her eyes.

—Sholom Aleichem, in his report for the *Jewish Immigration Bulletin,* 1917

ON THE SHIP CROSSING THE ATLANTIC

On board the ship we became utterly dejected. We were all herded together in a dark, filthy compartment in the steerage....Wooden bunks had been put up in two tiers...Seasickness broke out among us. Hundreds of people had vomiting fits....As all were crossing the ocean for the first time, they thought their end had come. The confusion of cries became unbearable.

ARRIVING IN AMERICA

"There is Ellis Island!" shouted an immigrant.... The name acted like magic. Faces grew taut, eyes narrowed. There, in those red buildings, fate awaited them. Were they ready to enter? Or were they to be sent back? "Only God knows," shouted an elderly man, his withered hand gripping the railing.

---

1. What are some words that come to your mind as you think about the experiences of immigrants as they leave home, travel, and arrive?

2. Why does Goldele—probably a teenager—have to stay in Antwerp? Why would her problem make it impossible for her to enter the United States with the rest of her family?

3. Why does the name Ellis Island act "like magic" on the immigrants? Taut faces and narrowed eyes are signs of worry. What were the immigrants worried about?

4. Why did immigrants undertake a voyage so filled with sadness and hardship? What did they hope to achieve?

Name: _____

Finishing a Script

When you read the exact words of an immigrant, you can find ways to respond as if you and the immigrant were actually talking and sharing. Read the script below. The words are those of Marcus Ravage, a Russian immigrant. Complete the script with your own responses to his words.

Marcus Ravage: In the evening when we were alone together my mother would... gaze into my eyes. "You will write us, dear?" she kept asking continually...

You: (Ask a <u>what</u> question and a <u>why</u> question.)

_____

_____

Marcus Ravage: At the moment of departure...she lost control of her feelings. As she embraced me for the last time her sobs became violent....There was a despair in her way of clinging to me which I could not then understand.

You: (Ask a couple of <u>why</u> questions.)

_____

_____

Marcus Ravage: I understand it now. I never saw her again.

You: (Ask a <u>why</u> question.)

_____

_____

Marcus Ravage: (Write the response Ravage might give to your <u>why</u> question above.)

_____

_____

Immigrants' Contributions

Y ou'll want your students to know the names and contributions of some "famous" immigrants. Just as important, you'll want students to see that the United States has been shaped by the contributions of immigrants whose names may not be famous, but whose culture and language have built our nation.

FAMOUS IMMIGRANTS AND THEIR LINES OF WORK

Talk with students about careers they envision for themselves. Then list some immigrants who have achieved success in these fields. Ask students to find the country of origin for each of these people. Then have students identify other fields and immigrants who succeeded in them.

The Performing Arts	**Irving Berlin, Mikhail Baryshnikov, Bob Hope, Bela Lugosi, Greta Garbo**
Law, Politics	**Abraham Beame, Edward Corsi, Emma Goldman, Felix Frankfurter, Marcus Garvey**
Science and Invention	**John Jacob Audubon, Albert Einstein, Enrico Fermi, John Muir, Elizabeth Blackwell**

Students will be interested to know that many of their favorite authors and illustrators are immigrants to the United States. As you present the following examples, ask how the writer's/illustrator's background is exhibited in the stories listed. See page 41 for a list of other authors who were immigrants.

Writer/Artist	Immigrant Background	Book(s)
Ludwig Bemelmans	**Born in Austria, 1898. Came to U.S. in 1914.**	*Madeline*
Esphyr Slobodkina	**Born in Siberia, 1908. Came to U.S. in 1928.**	*Caps for Sale*
Allen Say	**Born in Japan, 1937. Came to U.S in 1953.**	*El Chino Grandfather's Journey*
Maud and Miska Petersham	**Born 1890 and 1888 in Hungary. Came to U.S. in 1912.**	*The Poppy Seed Cakes*
Ed Young	**Born in China, 1931. Came to U.S. in 1951.**	*Lon Po Po, A Red-Riding Hood Story from China*

NAMES ON THE AMERICAN LAND

Read this paragraph aloud. Then use the discussion questions that follow it:

> There is no part of the world where nomenclature is so rich, poetical, humorous, and picturesque as the United States of America. All times, races, and languages have brought their contributions. Pekin is in the same State with Euclid, with Bellfontaine, and with Sandusky... The names of the States and territories themselves form a chorus of sweet and most romantic vocables: Delaware, Ohio, Indiana, Florida, Dakota, Iowa, Wyoming, Minnesota, and the Carolinas, there are few poems with a nobler music for the ear: a songful, tuneful land...
>
> — Robert Louis Stevenson, in *Across the Plains*, 1892

1. Why did Stevenson call the United States "a songful, tuneful, land"?

2. Pekin, Euclid, Bellfontaine, and Sandusky are all cities in Ohio, and their names come from four different languages: Chinese, Greek, French, and Polish. What does this tell you about immigrants and their final destinations? What did an immigrant from one country—say, Poland—have to adjust to as she or he met immigrants from other countries?

3. From coast to coast, the plurality of geographical names in the United States—names of states, mountains, rivers, lakes, etc.—are words from American Indian languages. How do you account for this?

4. Many U.S. place names from other languages are often clustered in a particular area or areas of the United States. For example, there are many Dutch place names in New York along the Hudson River, and many Spanish place names in California.

Distribute the reproducible on page 22, so that students can further explore how place names reflect the languages and settlement patterns of immigrants. After students complete the page, use the following prompts and questions to spur discussion:

✦ What does your completed map show you about the settlement patterns of the first European explorers and immigrants?

✦ Big parts of the map you completed are almost empty. This is because the map shows immigration only up to the mid-1800's. In the Westward Expansion after that time, many new communities were given English names. Why do you think this was so?

Analyzing Information

Immigrants brought many new words and names to the U.S. Find the following place names on the map. Use colored pencils or markers to underline the names.

1. Use red to underline these Spanish names: El Paso (TX), Santa Fe (NM), Pueblo (CO), Mesa (AZ), San Jose, Los Angeles, San Francisco, Sacramento (all in CA), Punta Gorda, St. Augustine, Carrabelle (all in FL).

2. Use green to underline these Dutch names: (all in NY) Yonkers, Peekskill, Watervliet, Amsterdam.

3. Use blue to underline these French names: New Orleans (LA), Louisville (KY), La Grange (GA), Bellefontaine (OH), Lapeer (MI), Marquette (MI), Terre Haute (IN).

4. Use orange to underline these German names: Stroudsberg (PA), Guttenberg (IO), Bismarck (ND), Rhinelander (WI).

5. Use yellow to underline these English names: Manchester (NH), Boston (MA), New York (NY), Baltimore (MD), Richmond (VA), Raleigh (NC), Charleston (SC), Philadelphia (PA), Hartford (CT).

6. What geographical patterns do the place names show? _____

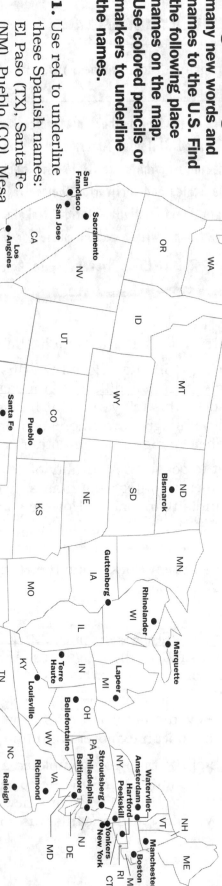

Scholastic Curriculum Guide: *Immigration*

Name: _____

Skills:
Synthesizing Information

Work with one or two partners. Read the questions below. Then use the facts and the graphs to help you decide on answers.

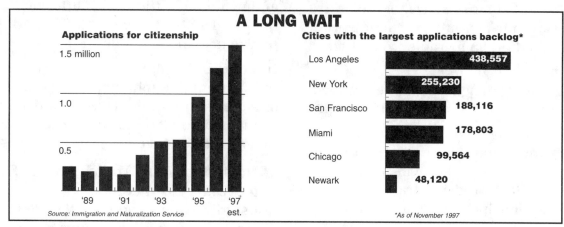

A LONG WAIT

Applications for citizenship

1.5 million

1.0

0.5

'89   '91   '93   '95   '97
                              est.

Source: Immigration and Naturalization Service

Cities with the largest applications backlog*

Los Angeles	438,557
New York	255,230
San Francisco	188,116
Miami	178,803
Chicago	99,564
Newark	48,120

*As of November 1997

FACTS

✦ In 1993, most immigrants were not seeking to become citizens.

✦ In 1995, new federal and state laws restricted benefits like welfare for immigrants. New laws threatened to deport some immigrants.

✦ Now more applications for citizenship are filed every year than in the years from 1911 to 1920.

✦ In 1996, it took an average of six months for an immigrant to become a citizen. In 1998, the average waiting time was 18 months and, in some cities, as much as three years.

1. According to the graph, in what year did the biggest jump in citizenship applications take place? _____

2. Why are so many more immigrants applying for citizenship? _____
_____

3. Where do most immigrants settle today? _____

4. How does the new procedure for becoming a citizen affect immigrants? affect Immigration Service offices? _____
_____

Cross-Curriculum Ideas

S tudents can continue their study of immigration in a variety of curriculum areas. Here are a few suggestions.

MATH: *State Statistics*

Students can search out statistics on the immigration patterns in their own state:

✦ The probable time of arrival of the first American Indian groups, the first Europeans, the first immigrants from other continents and nations.

✦ Immigrants settling in the state between 1840 and 1920, and after World War II.

✦ The approximate numbers of immigrants—and their countries of origin—entering the state in the past 10 years. Have students translate the data into timelines, pie charts, graphs, or diagrams.

SPORTS AND GAMES: *Play That Immigrated*

While many "all American" sports, such as baseball and basketball, originated in the United States, and many others—such as foot racing—have existed since time immemorial in almost all cultures, a great many sports and games "immigrated" to the U.S. Ask students to explore the national origins of games of physical skill, such as tennis, hockey, football, golf, and jai lai; and of mental games, such as dominoes, chess, Parcheesie, and checkers. Students might present their findings as sports-and-games illustrations on a world map, with all arrows leading to the U.S.A. Students might also demonstrate how to play some of these games.

HEALTH: *Can We Cure These Diseases?*

At Ellis Island and other ports-of-entry, doctors checked immigrants to see whether they suffered from infectious and contagious diseases. Those who did might be hospitalized at the entry station until cured, or deported. Students can research these diseases and report on their nature and symptoms, the possibilities of cure in the late 1800s and early 1900s, and their prevalence and rate of cure today.

trachoma, for instance, is an eye disease that is treatable today but was the cause of more than half of all medical detentions. Students can also research: **tuberculosis, favus, scarlet fever, diptheria, measles.**

LANGUAGE: *New World Words from Old World Sources*

Ask students to use adult dictionaries to find the origins of words we commonly use today and think of as part of our all-American "lingo." Present the words in groups. (Parentheses are for your information.) After students have found the origins of the words, you might challenge them to use them in "all American" sentences.

✦ yacht, sled, kink, waffle, hustle (Dutch)

✦ lotto, extravangaza, ballot, profile, ditto (Italian)

✦ ugly, wing, ill, slalom, cake, ski (Scandinavian)

✦ canasta, plaza, lasso, patio (Spanish)

✦ bungalow, kabob, thug, yoga (Hindi)

✦ sofa, ghoul, magazine (Arabic)

✦ kudos, myth, tonic, zinc, cosmetic (Greek)

✦ smuggle, snorkle, noodle, kindergarten (German)

✦ okra, gumbo, marimba, safari (African)

Scholastic Curriculum Guide: *Immigration*

Introduction to a Readers' Theater Play

On the following pages, you'll find a readers' theater play dramatizing the Ellis Island experiences of two immigrant families. By using the play, students can:

✦ bring their prior knowledge to an empathetic enactment of the immigrant experience

✦ practice speaking before small and large groups (a particularly valuable experience for quiet or at-risk students who need to build oral literacy)

TIPS FOR PREPARING FOR THE PLAY

Skim and Scan After passing out copies of the play, preview it with the class as a whole. Make sure students understand the formalities of a playscript: the list of characters, the typeface clues that indicate acts, scenes, and speakers. Have students identify the 13 speaking roles.

Set Up In a readers' theater play, actors sit on stools or chairs or stand in front of the audience and read their parts from the script. No costumes or sets are required. Props are not essential either, but most students will perform more easily if they have something to "handle" during the dramatization. For example, students playing inspectors and the doctor might have papers to shuffle; the student playing Ida Brodsky might hold a doll wrapped up as a baby; students playing Paulina, Ivan, Nicolai, and Stefan might hold suitcases or bags.

Cast Have students form two acting troupes. The play requires 13 actors. If you have more or less than 26 students, you have leeway with the number of actors playing Narrators or Inspectors. Let each troupe decide who will play the roles.

Rehearse Provide a quiet, private place for each troupe to read and rehearse the performance. Act as mentor by sitting in on rehearsals to offer suggestions and answer questions.

Performance If possible, have each troupe perform for the class on the same day or on two subsequent days. Back-to-back performances facilitate follow-up discussion. (See page 33 of this guide.)

Scholastic Curriculum Guide: *Immigration*

Name: _____

1912-1922 Immigration: First Stop, Ellis Island!

by Michael Peros

Characters (in order of appearance)

NARRATORS (1-2)

PAULINA SPIGOS: a Greek immigrant

IVAN ERDMAN: a Russian immigrant

NICOLAI ERDMAN: Ivan's son

INSPECTORS (1-4)

COMMISSIONER CURRAN

STEFAN BRODSKY: a Polish-American

IDA BRODSKY: Stefan's wife

DOCTOR

Edward Hausner / The New York Times Pictures

ACT 1

SCENE 1: 1912, IN NEW YORK HARBOR, ON THE DECK OF A BARGE APPROACHING ELLIS ISLAND

NARRATOR 1: Millions of people left Europe during the late 1800's. They fled their homes because of hunger, religious persecution, harsh governments, or the lack of jobs in their countries. Many had heard that the streets were paved with gold! From 1892 to 1954, Ellis Island was the first stop in America for many immigrants.

NARRATOR 2: Meet three new immigrants—Paulina Spigos and Ivan and Nicolai Erdman. They've already been checked for illnesses such as yellow fever, smallpox, and typhus. The ships they were on stopped in the lower part of the bay. Then doctors boarded the ships and checked the passengers. Now they're being taken by barge to Ellis Island.

PAULINA: The Statue of Liberty...she's so beautiful Can you see the lady?

IVAN: Thank you, yes.

NICOLAI (*to his father*): America! Everything will be fine now. Nothing bad will ever happen to us here.

SCENE 2: LATER THAT DAY. IN THE GREAT HALL ON ELLIS ISLAND.

NARRATOR 1: As the immigrants arrived, doctors studied the way they walked up the stairs to the Great Hall. (This was known as the "six-second medical.") Then the doctors would do a more thorough exam. After that, inspectors asked the immigrants a series of questions. Chances were—if you were a man in good health, with no criminal record, and good prospects for employment—you'd be allowed to enter America within a few hours.

NARRATOR 2: The rules, however, were more strict for women who were traveling alone, like Paulina.

INSPECTOR 1: Your full name is Paulina Spigos?

PAULINA: Yes sir, Paulina Spigos. I'm from Greece.

INSPECTOR 1: The doctors tell me you're in good health. You're single?

PAULINA: I'm engaged to be married, to Spiros Paniotis of Chicago.

INSPECTOR 1: Uh-huh. And you know this Spiros Paniotis of Chicago?

PAULINA (*indignantly*): Of course I know him. I grew up with him. He came here two years ago with his parents. He says he is ready for me to join him. Here, it says so in his letter.

INSPECTOR 1: Do I look like I can read Greek? He's meeting you here?

PAULINA: No, Chicago is too far away. He works.

INSPECTOR 1: Uh-huh. Since Chicago is too far away, how are you getting there?

PAULINA: I have money for a train ticket.

INSPECTOR 1: Uh-huh. Okay, Miss Spigos, only a few more questions—how much is five and five?

PAULINA: Ten.

INSPECTOR 1: How do you wash stairs? From the top or from the bottom?

PAULINA: With all respect sir, I did not come to America to wash stairs.

INSPECTOR 1: I see. Your Spiros is rich, is he? You'll have someone washing your stairs for you? Is this what your Spiros has told you? You see, Miss Spigos, this is exactly why we don't like to let women in by themselves.

PAULINA: I've known Spiros all my life. I know exactly what my life here in America will be like. Do you want to know what my life was like in Greece? Do you care that I had no family there?

INSPECTOR 1: Just calm down, Miss Spigos. We just don't want you falling into the wrong hands. But you seem like a woman who can take care of herself. Just be careful. You can change your money here for American dollars. You can buy your train ticket here, too. Next?

PAULINA: Inspector? The stairs? From the top to the bottom.

SCENE 3: SAME DAY. AN INSPECTOR'S OFFICE ON ELLIS ISLAND.

NARRATOR 1: About twenty percent of all immigrants were held for further questioning. About two percent of these were sent back to their home countries. People could be denied entry into the United States for a number of reasons: if they had criminal records, medical problems, or if they might not be able to support themselves.

NARRATOR 2: Sometimes families traveled all the way to America, only to be separated.

INSPECTOR 3: Mr. Erdman, why have you come to the United States?

IVAN: We had to. It was very hard for us in Russia.

NICOLAI: Inspector, we are Jewish. Last year, our family was forced to move. My father found it hard to work.

INSPECTOR 3: What was your business, Mr. Erdman?

IVAN: I was a tailor.

INSPECTOR 3: How much did you earn?

IVAN: About ten to twelve rubles.

INSPECTOR 3: Hmmm...that's about three dollars a week. Nicolai, what kind of work did you do?

NICOLAI: I was a student—until the government said I couldn't go to school anymore.

INSPECTOR 3 (*to Ivan*): Do you have a job waiting for you?

IVAN: No, Inspector. We know that it is against the law to have a job waiting for us. But, well, my brother Leon is here. He is a tailor, also.

INSPECTOR 3: What does he earn?

IVAN: About twelve rubles—I mean twelve dollars a week.

INSPECTOR 3: Does he have a family?

IVAN: A wife, and four children. May I sit down? It's been a very long day.

INSPECTOR 3: The doc says your fingers are stiff and swollen. Probably arthritis.

IVAN: No, no, it's nothing.

INSPECTOR 3: Nicolai, what are your plans in America?

NICOLAI: I am strong. There are many things I can do. My father will not have to work so hard here. I can take care of him.

INSPECTOR 3: You have twenty-three dollars between you. Your father is a tailor, but look at his hands—he can't work. And Nicolai, you have no job experience at all. Do you know how many young, strong men come into this country every day? I'm sorry.

(*The inspector marks the letters "SI" on the shoulder of Ivan's coat.*)

NICOLAI: "SI?" What is this?

INSPECTOR 3: Special inquiry. It means your father will be deported, sent back to Russia.

NICOLAI: But they will kill him! No! No, you cannot send him back!

IVAN: Nicolai, do not say anything.

NICOLAI: Papa, I am not like you. I cannot say yes to everything. (*To the inspector*) I will take care of him. I will earn enough money for both of us to live!

INSPECTOR 3 (*shrugging*): Maybe you can convince the Board of Special Inquiry?

NICOLAI: What is that?

INSPECTOR 3: You can explain your situation to three inspectors. They'll give you a translator if you want one. They'll decide whether your father can stay. Next!

IVAN: Nicolai, we have been here a number of days. We have talked to so many people. I'm tired....

NICOLAI: Papa—

IVAN: Look at my hands. They're right. I can't work the way I did.

NICOLAI: You cannot go back to Russia!

IVAN: It's my home, Nicolai. Just as America will be your home.

NICOLAI: Please, Papa—

IVAN: No. My mind is made up. Now—go to the inspector. Tell him I want to return to Russia. I want to go home.

ACT 2

SCENE 1: 1922. IN THE GREAT HALL OF ELLIS ISLAND.

NARRATOR 1: Between 1901 and 1910, over seven million immigrants entered the United States through Ellis Island. The numbers dropped during World War I. But after the war ended in 1918, the numbers started rising. As a result, the First Quota Law was passed in 1921. This put a monthly limit on the number of immigrants who could enter the United States from any given country.

NARRATOR 2: Stefan Brodsky, a Polish-American man who immigrated to the United States two years earlier, is pacing in the Great Hall. He stops long enough to stare at the faces of the new arrivals entering the Great Hall. Commissioner Curran, who is in charge of Ellis Island, approaches Stefan.

CURRAN: Good afternoon. Are you waiting for someone?

STEFAN: Yes, my wife Ida, Ida Brodsky. She's coming from Poland. Her ship's a day late.

CURRAN: How long have you been in America?

STEFAN: Oh, we've both been here for two years. Ida only went back to visit her parents. Her mother's sick. I only hope everything is all right.

CURRAN: No need to worry. I'm Commissioner Curran, and I can assure you that these little trips don't count against the Quota Law.

STEFAN: Thank you, Mr. Curran, but you don't understand—

CURRAN: You see, if your wife has already been admitted to the United States, and then she goes back to her homeland—well, when she returns to America, she'll probably be allowed in. Even if Poland's limit has already been reached.

(*Ida Brodsky, carrying a bundle, enters the Great Hall. She is accompanied by the ship's doctor and an inspector.*)

STEFAN: I realize that, but you—

IDA: Stefan!

STEFAN: Ida!

CURRAN: What's that she's carrying?

STEFAN: I believe that's our baby. Excuse me, Commissioner (*hurrying up to Ida*).

IDA: Stefan, look. He has your eyes.

DOCTOR: Mrs. Brodsky needs to stay here in the hospital tonight so I can check her out. The baby was born just last night.

IDA: Stefan, there's a problem—

STEFAN: What? What is it? Are you all right? The baby? What?

IDA: No, nothing like that.

INSPECTOR 4: The Polish quota was reached yesterday. To put it bluntly—the mother can stay, but the baby must leave.

IDA: My baby! They can't send my baby away!

STEFAN: Don't worry, Ida. No one will take our baby.

CURRAN: Are you sure the quota has been reached?

INSPECTOR 4: Yes, sir.

IDA: Stefan, if our baby can't come in, I will go back to Poland with him.

STEFAN: Mr. Curran. Please, help us.

CURRAN: Don't worry, Stefan, I'm sure we can work this out. (*to the Inspector*) Where was the baby born?

INSPECTOR 4: Aboard ship, sir. On the *Lapland*, of the British Star Line.

CURRAN: There you are! The baby wasn't born in Poland, but on a British ship. The deck of a British ship, no matter where in the world it is, is the same as British soil. Include the baby in the British quota.

INSPECTOR 4: Sir...the British quota was reached yesterday.

IDA: Our baby can't come in?

CURRAN: Wait, wait. You said the baby was born on board the Lapland? That ship's home port is Belgium. There! The baby is Belgian!

STEFAN: My baby is what?

INSPECTOR 4: Uh...sir? The Belgian quota ran out a week ago.

CURRAN: Inspector, whose side are you on?

INSPECTOR 4: Sorry, sir, just doing my job.

STEFAN: First my baby's Polish, then he's British, then he's Belgian. Now what is he?

CURRAN: Look here, I've got it. You see, with children, it's the way it is with wills. We follow the intention.

STEFAN AND IDA: What?

INSPECTOR 4: What?

CURRAN: Here's the thing. It's clear enough that Ida was hurrying back so that the baby would be born in America. And the baby had the same intention—he wanted to be born in America. But the ship was a day late, and that upset everything. So, under the law, this baby, by intention, was born in America. This baby is definitely an American.

IDA: Stefan. (*whispering to her husband*) What's your first name, Mr. Curran?

STEFAN: We'd like to name our baby after you.

THE END

Follow-Up Activities for the Play

H ere are a few ways to extend students' learning after they read the play *1912-1922 Immigration: First Stop, Ellis Island!*

RULES AND REGULATIONS
Guide the class in an exploration of the following issues:

✦ The first act of the play is set in 1912. What were the big tests that immigrants had to pass at that time? (*health; some money; intelligence; support; place to go*)

✦ What was the 1921 "quota law"? (*monthly limit on number of immigrants from any given country*) How did this affect families who wanted to travel together to the United States?

✦ What were the responsibilities of the different inspectors at Ellis Island and other entry points? What special challenges did they have to face? How did Curran "get around" the rules?

MAKING "EDUCATED GUESSES"
Encourage students to make "educated guesses" about these questions: Are there regulations that affect immigration to the United States today? What do you think they are? How could you check out your educated guesses?

TRACKING TRENDS
Explore these points with the class:

✦ Ivan intended to stay with his brother. Pauline would live with her husband-to-be. Like most immigrants to major U.S. cities, these two characters intended to settle down with people from their home countries. This was typical of new immigrants. Settlement patterns in cities gave rise to terms like Little Italy, Chinatown, and German Town. What are some reasons why immigrants gathered together to form small communities within large cities? (*a common language; culture; poverty; prejudice from established Americans*) Ask students to identify immigrant nicknames for parts of your community or state.

✦ First- and second-generation Americans (immigrants' children born in the United States) have tended to move away from ethnic neighborhoods. Why do you think this is so? (*more money; learning English; feeling "American" rather than a member of some other nation*)

Scholastic Curriculum Guide: *Immigration*

Using Literature Circles

A literature circle is an effective way to help students select and appreciate fiction and nonfiction works. A small group works together, selecting, studying, and discussing the same books. Students can exchange ideas and gain new insights from each other. The following suggestions can help you establish literature circles for your study of immigration.

1. Have at-the-ready and display on a table several books about the immigrant experience. Aim for a balanced list of fiction and nonfiction. (See page 48 for a starter list.) As you hold up each book, give the title, author's name, genre (fiction or nonfiction), and a brief teaser about the book's contents.

2. Give each student a sign-up index card with these sections for the student to fill in: *My Name; Three Books I Want To Read; Why I Want To Read Them.* Ask students to fill in the cards as they examine more closely the books you've displayed.

3. Collect the cards and do your own juggling— based on the card information— to find common interests; choose three or four books (fiction, nonfiction, or both) for each circle, and assign students to each circle. In this way, you'll assure that students of different abilities and backgrounds have an opportunity to work together on subjects of mutual interest.

4. Provide the groups with focus questions to guide their reading and discussions. You'll find literature circle discussion cards for three books on pages 35-37. Note that the cards for *If Your Name Was Changed at* *Ellis Island* and *Immigrant Kids* assume that students have read the whole book before they begin their discussion, while the cards for *Dragon's Gate* call for discussion after each group of chapters.

5. With the class, write and post some guidelines for effective discussion. Examples:

✦ Give each group member a chance to speak.

✦ Take turns. Don't interrupt.

✦ Listen carefully to what each member of your group is saying.

✦ Present your own ideas as clearly and briefly as possible. Use any disagreement as a chance to learn! Find ways to blend conflicting ideas into a Big Picture about the books and the questions they raise.

6. As you sit in on group discussions now and then, use your background and your familiarity with each book to reorient groups that get bogged down in details, lapse into silences, or fly off into tangents. The models and prompts you offer to groups will help students learn how to conduct literature circles productively and to learn a lot from them.

Name: _____

Literature Circle Cards for
If Your Name Was Changed at Ellis Island

If Your Name Was Changed at Ellis Island

Card 1

How is the book organized? How does this organization help you find the facts you want?

If Your Name Was Changed at Ellis Island

Card 2

Which two sections of the book are most informative to you? What are the most important things you learned from these sections?

If Your Name Was Changed at Ellis Island

Card 3

What questions do you have about immigration that are not answered in the book? Where might you find the answers to your questions?

If Your Name Was Changed at Ellis Island

Card 4

Which description or section in the book leaves you with an especially strong feeling, such as anger, pride, sadness, or happiness? Point out some of the words and phrases that build the feeling.

If Your Name Was Changed at Ellis Island

Card 5

After reading this book, what would you like to find out about your own family's immigrant background?

If Your Name Was Changed at Ellis Island

Card 6

With whom would you like to share this book? Why?

Cut along dotted lines

Name: _____

Literature Circle Cards for
Immigrant Kids

Immigrant Kids

Card 1

How is this book illustrated? How do the pictures provide information about the lives of immigrant kids?

Immigrant Kids

Card 2

Imagine that you suddenly time-travel to an immigrant neighborhood in a big city in 1910. What would be the hardest thing for you to get used to about the neighborhood? What would seem familiar, or something like kids' lives today?

Immigrant Kids

Card 3

What are the major differences between your school and the schools attended by immigrant kids? In what ways are the schools the same?

Immigrant Kids

Card 4

Why did so many immigrant children leave school and get jobs? Kids today can also work to earn money. So what's the big difference between you as a paid worker today and an immigrant kid as a paid worker in 1910?

Immigrant Kids

Card 5

What are some games that immigrant kids played? Who organized the games? How are the games different from the ones you play today? How are they the same? What do the games tell you about the times they are played in?

Immigrant Kids

Card 6

In your opinion, what are the three most important ideas in this book? Review all the chapters before you answer.

Cut along dotted lines

Name: _____

Literature Circle Cards for
Dragon's Gate

Dragon's Gate

Card 1

Preface; Chapters 1-6
(Preface, and pages 1-52)

- **Why are Otter's father and uncle heroes in their home town in China?**
- **Why does Otter's mother want him to stay home?**
- **What event makes it necessary for Otter to leave?**

Dragon's Gate

Card 2

Chapters 7-12 (pages 53-113)

- **If you were painting a picture of the railroad workers' environment, what would you emphasize? Why?**
- **What is Otter's reaction to his father's and uncle's situation at the camp? Why does he feel this way?**

Dragon's Gate

Card 3

Chapters 13-18 (pages 114-162)

- **In what way are Otter's and Sean's fathers alike? How do they affect their sons' friendship?**
- **Why do the Outsiders quarrel with one another? How does Otter get them to work together?**

Dragon's Gate

Card 4

Chapters 19-24 (pages 163-214)

- **What happens when Otter tells Kilroy he's going home? What other master-servant relationship does this incident remind you of?**
- **What bargain does Otter strike with Kilroy? What are Foxfire's and Sean's reasons for joining Otter?**

Dragon's Gate

Card 5

Chapters 25-30 (pages 215-272)

- **Why do Otter's feelings about his uncle change?**
- **What happens as a result of Otter's discovery about the working conditions of T'ang men?**
- **How will Otter's experiences in America affect him?**

Dragon's Gate

Card 6

Summing Up

- **What does the Dragon's Gate symbolize?**
- **What does Otter write in the soil? What do you think these words mean?**

Cut along dotted lines

Responding to Literature

Have students try one or more of these activities after they've read their literature circle's book.

CHANGE THE STORY

If students have read a fiction book, have them write an alternate ending. They can use the situations, problems, and characters in the original story, but write a final chapter to show how things might have ended up differently.

ADD A NEW CHARACTER

Suggest that students cast themselves as a character in the story. Remind them to use <u>I</u> and <u>me</u> as they rewrite a chapter, section, or some paragraphs from the book to show their part in the events and how the events are affecting them.

A CHARACTER CORRESPONDENCE

Have students imagine that two immigrants from different books and different times can send letters to one another. Students should write letters in which the characters share ideas, tell about their experiences, and perhaps give advice to one another.

A DIFFERENT AUDIENCE

Students might rewrite the story for a younger child. Explain that they should retell the main ideas in a simple way. They might draw pictures to make some of the ideas clear to their young audience.

BOOK CRITICS

Have students choose two books they've read and write a book review that compares and contrasts the books. Students should give the books' titles and authors, say what the books are about, tell whether they are fiction or nonfiction, and explain how they are alike and how they are different. Ask students to end with their opinions: Which book taught them more about immigrants and immigration? Which book was more fun and interesting to read? Why?

STORY PANELS

Have students identify the most important events and incidents in a book they've read about immigration, then make a picture-story panel to show these events. Suggest that students include dialogue balloons or captions to accompany each panel.

Using Poetry

The following poem can help students review concepts about the immigrant experience and, at the same time, help them review some of the elements of poetry. Read the poem aloud to the class, then use the queastions to promote discussion.

AMERICA!
Fanya Albert: Ellis Island, March 7, 1911

Soon the Golden Land would welcome them,
the first-class passengers,
the ones with cabins.
From behind the metal gate,
I could glimpse fragments:

     a billowing feather on a hat,

     a silk scarf,

     a tapered hand in pale suede,

     an elegant carrying case.

They would go straight to the city.

Not us. Not the steerage.

     Feathers?

Ours, if any, had been sewn into quilts.
We had no suede gloves,

     no silk—

just babushkas and bundles,
hopes and prayers.
First we must go to Ellis Island.

We waited.
A human jumble:
babies crying, elders sighing,
our ears swimming in a noisy stew
of German, Italian, Swedish, Yiddish,
even English with an Irish lilt.
We did not understand each other's words,
except one—
America!

At last the gate swung open,
and we crowded into the ferry.
Then, as it pulled away from the ship,
we saw her—Lady Liberty!
A goddess
rising from the sea,
her strong arm holding a torch
as if to light our way.
One by one we whispered the word,
      "America!"
         "America!"
Again and again,
       "America!"
      "America!"
until
      the echoed word became a blizzard!
A swarm of sparkling jewels that I could see
         hovering
      over the dark water.

Minutes later,
the ferry docked at Ellis Island.
Looking at us,
a worn and shabby crowd,
could anyone tell?
Could anyone know
we each carried a treasure?
It was a single precious word—
     America!
          —Bobbi Katz

QUESTIONS ABOUT THE IMMIGRANT EXPERIENCE

✦ Who is the speaker in the poem? In what section of the ship is she traveling?

✦ Who else is on the ship? What is a *first class* passenger?

✦ Why don't the passengers understand one another?

✦ Who is Lady Liberty? Why does the sight of her pull passengers together?

ABOUT ELEMENTS OF POETRY

✦ "America" doesn't have lines that rhyme. What, then, makes it a poem?

✦ The poem has many word pictures, like "billowing feathers on a hat." What are some other word pictures in the poem?

✦ Most poems leave readers with a feeling. What feelings do you have after hearing this poem?

Projects

As part of your Immigration unit, students can work on group or individual projects. These pages present some project ideas. Students can use the reproducibles on page 43 and 44 to organize their research and to plan a schedule for carrying it out.

Anthology of Interviews Students can interview family members and neighbors to collect handed-down anecdotes and firsthand recollections of immigrant experiences. Review the quotations on pages 4 and 18 as examples of the kinds of stories that students might note or tape-record in the interviews. As an alternative to a written anthology, students might reenact the interviews with classmates in the class's Interview Center (page 9).

Talk About Our Times Partners can write and present as readers' theater a dialogue between an immigrant of long ago and a recent immigrant. In the dramatization, the characters can compare and contrast facts and ideas about where they came from, why they came, what they are seeking, and the hurdles and challenges they must overcome as they seek to settle down in the United States.

Immigrant Issues Students might research and then debate some current issues related to immigration. Possible questions might include:

✦ Should immigration to the United States be restricted and controlled?

✦ Should immigrants who are not citizens get the same benefits as citizens do?

Debate teams, perhaps two on each side of the issue, need not follow strictly Roberts' Rules of Order. But each side should attend to the following guidelines, which you can present ahead of time:

✦ Collect lots of facts together to support your position. (This is the key guideline for debators. Facts, not opinions, will support the argument.)

✦ In a debate, debators take turns speaking, and don't interrupt one another.

✦ To prepare for a debate, try to predict what your opponents' counter-arguments are likely to be so that you can respond to them in your replies.

✦ Follow this pattern:

Team One, First Speaker: Present your team's point of view.

Team Two, First Speaker: Present your team's point of view.

Team One, Second Speaker: Restate your team's point of view, then state

some reasons why you think Team Two's first speaker's reasons don't hold up.

Team Two, Second Speaker: Restate your team's point of view, then state some reasons that contradict the arguments of Speaker Two on Team One.

In Conclusion: A speaker from each team summarizes the team's main point of view and the supporting facts.

The classroom audience should listen to assess the preciseness of the facts presented and the presentation skills of the debators (clarity, sticking to the point). Some members of the audience may change their opinions about the issue as a result of the debate, but this is not the main goal. Instead, it is to consider immigration issues from different angles. After the formal debate, audience members can tell what they learned, how the speakers affected them, and what else they'd like to learn about the topic.

Future Immigration Pose questions such as these to the class: Who will be the immigrants to the moon or to another planet? Why would they want to immigrate to these distant places? What skills might they have to have? What will they want to take with them? What work will they do in such a new environment? What nations might participate? Challenge students to use facts and concepts they've learned about immigration on planet Earth to make educated guesses about realistic motives, rules, and problems that galactic explorers and immigrants might have to deal with. Students can work independently or with a partner to present their ideas in written or oral reports, realistic short stories, or personal logs which record an immigrant's experience.

Mini-Biographies Students can research to learn about the immigrant background and United States experiences of well-known creators of young people's books. Independently or with a partner, students can aim for an anthology of five or more one-to-two-paragraph biographies. Suggest that students conclude their anthologies with an appendix listing the titles of best-known books by the authors and illustrators. Get students started by re-presenting the list on page 20 and expanding the first column there with the following:

Roger Duvoisin	Anita Lobel	Leo Lionni	Tomi Ungerer
H.A. Rey	Antonio Frasconi	David Macaulay	Peter Sis
Peter Spier	Eve Bunting	Ingri and Edgar Parin d'Aulaire	

Name: _____

Project Research Form

MY TOPIC IS _____

MY GOAL IN DOING THIS PROJECT IS TO SHOW _____

_____

THE MAIN QUESTIONS I WANT MY REPORT TO ANSWER ARE _____

_____

_____

MY RESEARCH SOURCES (Fill in titles as you do your research.)

Books
_____

_____

_____

Magazine and Newspaper Articles
_____

_____

_____

Internet/Web Sites
_____

_____

_____

Movies, Videos, Filmstrips
_____

_____

_____

Visits to People and Places
_____

_____

Special Discoveries
_____

_____

Name: _____

PROJECT ORGANIZER:
Tasks and Time

Make a timetable to help you plan and carry out your project.

My topic: _____

Form in which I'll present my project:_____

Number of days I have to complete my project: _____

TASK: DOING RESEARCH

❏ Collect resources   Date: _____

❏ Take notes   Date: _____

❏ Conduct interviews   Date: _____

❏ Make visits   Date: _____

TASK: ORGANIZING INFORMATION

❏ Put notes in order   Date: _____

❏ Organize visuals: pictures,   Date: _____
    maps, graphs, photos

❏ Make an outline   Date: _____

TASK: DRAFTING AND REVISING

❏ Write my first draft   Date: _____

❏ Confer with partner   Date: _____

❏ Confer with teacher   Date: _____

❏ Revise draft, make final copy   Date: _____

TASK: PRESENTING/PUBLISHING

❏ Fine-tune my presentation   Date: _____

❏ Present it to classmates   Date: _____

In Conclusion

REVISIT THE K-W-L CHARTS

Have students return to the K-W-L charts that they started at the beginning of the unit. Ask them to complete the last colum of these charts and to revise any misconceptions that they had in the first column.

REVIEW WITH A BOARD GAME

To review facts and concepts about immigration, have students design a serious board game in which the object is to move from Start (another country) to the Goal, the United States. Because—like immigration itself—the path on a board game (for example, Monopoly) entails theme-specific steps, stops, obstacles, penalties, and rewards, the planning of such a game gives students an opportunity to show precisely what they now know about the challenges immigrants face to reach their goals. You can act as scribe at the chalkboard, drawing a "first draft" of the game board and incorporating the class's suggestions about the words for various path-steps. Then, encourage students to form groups to actually construct the board game, revising and fine tuning the chalkboard model, writing and testing directions, and then showing classmates how to play the final version.

A NATIONAL TREE

Briefly review with students what a picture of a family tree shows, then have students suggest how to adapt the idea to draw a National Tree showing the many different groups of immigrants that have come to make up the United States. To get the activity going, you can act as artist/scribe at the chalkboard. Draw the tree trunk and label it United States. As you draw the lowest (oldest) branches, ask students to tell what first immigrants these branches represent. Continue with smaller branches going upward to represent the immigrant groups arriving in the 1800's, then those arriving in the early 1900s, then those arriving most recently. Leave some of the branches unlabelled for students to fill in when they draw their own versions of the National Tree.

Invite students to use the chalkboard sketch as a starter-upper for their own renditions of the National Tree. Encourage accurate, information-loaded embellishments, such as branches colored like national flags and leaves bearing names of famous immigrants from a specific country. To encourage the making of large, colorful, and informative trees, explain that the final products will be displayed as a mural on a classroom wall.

Scholastic Curriculum Guide: *Immigration*

Assessment Suggestions

D uring their study of immigration, students will be involved in a wide range of activities. Here are some ways to assess and evaluate students' progress.

ASSESSMENTS BY THE TEACHER

You don't have time—nor is there any need—to formally evaluate every item of each student's work. Instead, keep a simple Start, Midway, Conclude chart for each student, and use spot checks like these to fill in the charts at three points as your class moves through the unit.

✦ Listen to a student's questions—whether posed in whole-class discussions, in study and project groups, or to you as a mentor—to assess what that student seems to know initially, how her/his knowledge is building, and how well the student has grasped the major concepts about immigration. Remember: great, thought-provoking questions indicate knowledge, curiosity, and enthusiasm.

✦ From time to time, call eight or ten students together in roundup groups to discuss achievements and challenges they're experiencing as they work through the unit activities. While you act as group mentor and guide, you can also detect problems that individual students may be having and ways they are seeking to solve them.

ASSESSMENTS BY CLASSMATES

Students can work together to create pre-activity criteria for assessing the outcome of their work on the various activities in the unit. Write the class's standards on poster paper and leave them on display. When activities are completed, students can form small groups, share work, and use the standards as they discuss and assess their work.

- Shows a lot of research done with many sources.
- The main ideas are clearly presented.
- Each main idea is supported with details.

SELF-ASSESSMENTS

We're all our own best critics. This is certainly true of students, who learn more about their own work by reading it to or telling about it aloud to a small group of classmates. Make this process, called a Free-Read or a Free-Tell, an ongoing activity as your students move through this unit. Each student can keep a simple log in which to record her/his own perceptions after sharing work aloud.

What I Read
A script of my interview with an immigrant from Hong Kong.

What I Like About It
I like the way I let the person I interviewed do most of the talking.

What I Want to Change
I think I left in a lot of details that don't stick to the subject. I think I want to take these details out when I revise.

Answers to Reproducibles

M ost reproducibles in this teaching guide encourage students to respond and react in individual, original ways. The answers below are for reproducibles that check students' skills in interpretation and application of factual data.

Page 11: Using a Graph and Chart 1. 12 2. Europe 3. the Americas; Europe 4. Sample response: The graph would show many Americans whose national origin was in Asia, or the Americas.

Page 14: Clues to Use Puzzle Sentences will vary. Possible answers are given. 2. native/Many immigrants have ties to their native land. 3. immigrated/Ellis Island was a gate to those who immigrated. 4. alien/ Can an alien always get in? 5. green card/ To get a green card, it is helpful to read English. 6. Angel Island/ Once, ships from Asia would land at Angel Island. 7. emigrated/Many people emigrated because there wasn't enough to eat in their homelands. 8. naturalization/After going through the naturalization process, it will be your turn to become a citizen. 9. persecution/Some people had to run from persecution in their native lands.

Page 22: Analyzing Information 1-5 Check to be sure that students complete the maps correctly. 6. Correctly completed maps will show these patterns: Spanish (red): Texas, New Mexico, Colorado, Arizona, California, Florida; Dutch (green): New York; French (blue): Louisiana, Kentucky, Georgia, Ohio, Michigan, Indiana; German (orange):Pennsylvania, Iowa, North Dakota, Wisconsin; English (yellow): New Hampshire, Massachusetts, New York, Maryland, Virginia, North Carolina, South Carolina, Pennsylvania, Connecticut

Page 23: Synthesizing Information Sample responses: 1.1995; 2. New laws can cut off benefits to people who are not citizens and make them fear they'll be sent back to their home countries. 3. They settle in major cities. 4. Immigrants must wait much longer to become citizens. Immigration Service offices in major cities are backed up with citizenship applications.

More Immigration Materials From Scholastic

PICTURE BOOKS

Dooley, Norah. *Everybody Cooks Rice* (ages 4-8)

Gomi, Taro. *My Father* (ages 4-7)

Ortiz, Fran. *Hello, Amigos!* (ages 6-10)

Levine, Ellen. *I Hate English!* (ages 6-8)

Surat, Michele Maria. *Angel Child, Dragon Child* (ages 6-9)

FICTION

Denenberg, Barry. *So Far from Home: The Diary of Mary Driscoll, an Irish Mill Girl* (ages 9-14)

Kerr, Judith. *When Hitler Stole Pink Rabbit* (ages 8-12)

Levitan, Sonia. *Journey to America* (ages 8-12)

Lord, Bette Bao. *In the Year of the Boar and Jackie Robinson* (ages 8-12)

Porter, Connie. *Happy Birthday, Kristen!* (ages 8-12)

Sachs, Marilyn. *Call Me Ruth* (ages 8-12)

Sandin, Joan. *The Long Way to a New Land* (ages 6-10)

Stevens, Carla. *Lily and Miss Liberty* (ages 7-10)

Yep, Laurence. *Dragon's Gate* (ages 9-14)

Yep, Laurence. *The Star Fisher* (ages 8-12)

NONFICTION

Bode, Janet. *New Kids in Town: Oral Histories of Immigrant Teens* (ages 10 up)

Bunting, Eve. *Train to Somewhere* (ages 7-10)

Freedman, Russell. *Immigrant Kids* (ages 8-12)

Goldsmith, Diane. *Hoang Anh* (ages 8-12)

Levine, Ellen. *If Your Name Was Changed at Ellis Island* (7-10)

Maestro, Betsy. *Coming to America* (ages 5-9)

Murphy, Jim. *Across America on an Emigrant Train* (ages 9 up)

Warren, Andrea. *Orphan Train Rider: One Boy's True Story* (ages 8-10)

SCHOLASTIC PROFESSIONAL RESOURCE BOOKS

Baiker, Karen. *Immigration Then and Now*

TECHNOLOGY

Smart Books: If Your Name Was Changed at Ellis Island